Copyright © 2015 Joshu

First Edition

All rights reserved.

ISBN-13:
978-1519128010

ISBN-10:
1519128010

No part of this publication may be reproduced, stored in a retrieval system or transmitted in any form or by any means, electronic, mechanical, photocopying, recording, scanning or otherwise, except under the terms of the Copyright, Designs and Patents Act 1988 or under the terms of a license issued by the Copyright Licensing Agency Ltd.

Legal Disclaimer

The Publisher and the Author make no representations or warranties with respect to the accuracy or completeness of the contents of this work and specifically disclaim all warranties, including without limitation warranties for a particular purpose. No warranty may be created or extended by sales or promotional materials. The advice and strategies contained herein may not be suitable for every situation.

Neither the publisher nor the author shall be liable for damages arising here from. The fact that an organization or website is referred to in this work as a citation and/or a potential source of further information does not mean that the author or the publisher endorses the information the organization or website may provide or recommendations it may make.

Further, readers should be aware that Internet websites listed in this work may have changed or disappeared between when this work was written and when it is read.

Dedicated to those incredible teachers, parents, students, counselors, and college admission professionals who contributed greatly to the content of this important book.

Section

01

What Good Can Come Of This?
What Bad Can Come Of This?
(It's All About Choices)

Chapter 1

Decisions, Decisions and More Decisions

Welcome to high school. The next four years of your life are absolutely going to be a blast. You are going to make new friends. You are going to learn new things. And you just might set yourself up for an incredible life of success and happiness.

However, for most freshman students, the only future they think about is next week's quiz, tonight's homework, or Friday's football game. But thriving freshman are different. They are in fact, thinking about their futures. They are thinking about next year's classes. They are already thinking about the college application process and they are thinking about the kind of life they wish to live when all this school stuff is over.

By way of introduction, my name is Chadney Hill. My brother Joshua and I wrote this book to give students like you (frankly, students like us) a better understanding of the importance of the freshman year. I started on this book when I was just a junior in High School and Joshua was just a measly seventh grader. Our goal is to change the common narrative that the first year of high school is really not that important. Some of our classmates have even said that college admission officers don't even look at the freshman year. It simply isn't true.

> *"Lots of colleges, particularly private schools, will look at the freshman year. And since your academic performance as a freshman influences what classes you'll be able to take as a sophomore, it matters for pretty much every college. So don't panic if you have a stumble here or there while learning the ropes of high school. But don't blow off your freshman year, either."*
>
> *Kevin McMullin founder and head of counseling at Collegewise*

We aren't trying to stress you out, but we are trying to give you a sense of the urgency and competitiveness that exists this year whether you know it or not. The fact is, that thriving students build tremendous momentum in their freshman years. We have studied, researched and interviewed dozens and dozens of high performing high school students and the reality is that you can look at their achievements and performance during their freshman year and predict with great certainty their future high school success. We don't have to tell you (but we will) that the formula for high school success is pretty simple and you can see it in these high performing students; they get excellent grades, they turn their assignments in on time, they don't miss classes, they make friends, and they get involved.

Make no mistake about it, success in high school is deliberate. It takes effort, strategy, and execution. Most importantly, it requires the right attitude. One of the most common things we heard in our interviews from students is that there is a perception that some kids (the academic super stars) are just naturally smart. But when you really look at the academic super stars what you discover is that those kids work their butts off to get those top grades. Our conclusion is that those kids aren't naturally smarter. In fact, during the learning process, they receive the same information at the same time as other students. If they have a gift, it's a gift of focus. We believe that a students focus is largely determined by the students attitude about studying. The students we talked to have a very mature understanding of why education and good grades is important to their future success. They have already set their mind on going to college and perhaps most importantly, they know that they are in a competition for the relatively small number of spots available at their dream college.

You have to have an attitude that is centered on winning. Winning needs to be defined academically and socially. It will be based upon your goals, hopes, and dreams. But the practical aspect of having a winning attitude means you are prepared (intellectually, physically, emotionally...etc.) to sacrifice to win. So if you need to get a 4.2 GPA to get into your dream college or to secure that scholarship, then you must develop the discipline to do the extra work. Too many students, especially freshman students, get so caught up in the incredible social opportunities surrounding high school that they fail to achieve their academic goals which ultimately could result in them not achieving their life dreams.

As you begin your freshman journey it is essential that you stay focused on the outcome you are hoping to achieve these next four years. Specifically, you want to position yourself to excel in life. We take the perspective that every student reading this book has a similar dream of wanting to live an extraordinary life filled with success and happiness. If you recognize that the first post-high school step to this new life of incredible possibilities begins with college than you are already thinking correctly. Now you need to begin to develop the mindset that there is no question that you will be going to college. Therefore, every decision you make from here on out will be measured against the impact that decision will have against your college goal.

THRIVING FRESHMAN TIP #1

Measure Every Decision To Spend Out-Of-Class Time On Social Activities Against The Question, "Will This Activity Prevent Me From Delivering A Stellar Performance On My Academic Assignments Today Or This Week?"

If the answer is either maybe or yes, then you need... you *must* muster up the self-discipline to either skip the activity or reschedule the activity. This is likely going to require you to develop a new skill, a skill that most people don't have... self-discipline. Think about all the people in the world that start diets and then quit within a few days or weeks. How about all the people who join gyms only to stop going before their first month's membership is even billed. For these people, the idea of going to the gym is more painful than the morning glance in the mirror… where they see their less-than-ideal body. But people who do stick to diets or fitness plans are people with discipline. So how do you develop self-discipline? Well, there is a whole body of research on this subject, but it basically boils down to one thing. People activate changes in their lives when the pain of doing the same thing becomes greater than the pain of pursuing the change. So, if you are the kind of student who thinks studying is more painful (emotionally) than hanging out with friends or video games then you need to flip the pain switch.

You have to make your personal pain of under-performing in school higher than the pain of missing out on this week's party.

> "The student's friends may pressure them to not study and instead come hang out with them and have fun, but that is the student's decision to make. At some point in their high school careers, every student must decide what their priorities will generally be. Will they prioritize their social life over their classes, or will it be the reverse? Whatever they decide, each student has control over their own actions and decisions. Students should never let someone else take the reins for them just

because they consider the other person to be a friend."

(Marissa Nardella, high school student)

For this to happen, you have to get educated. You have to develop a solid understanding of why performing well in school is so critical to your future success. This book will help you obtain that knowledge.

But you already know this, right? Your common sense tells you that the higher you perform academically the greater the chances of getting into a dream college. Your instincts tell you that the better the college the better the future opportunities. Everybody understands this… right? So then why do so many kids allow themselves to struggle and under-perform? We think the answer is pretty simple… they are busy, blind and distracted.

Busy students may not have the time management skills to perform at a high level. Blind students (basically, every freshman who does not yet know or who has not yet become acclimated to high school standards) struggle to perform because they just don't have the information necessary to succeed. Distracted kids lack the discipline to focus on performing well.

The good news is, all of these things are easily managed and this book is going to give you the information and strategies to perform.

Everything in this book is based on first-hand experiences. The advice we offer comes from more than 100 sources, including high school counselors, college admission officers, students, teachers, and parents. There are a ton of kids out there who will do well without this information. However, kids who just do well don't go to awesome colleges. The world is way too competitive for students who achieve "typical" or "average" results. To thrive in life you must thrive in high school. We want you to thrive. By the way, thriving doesn't mean sitting in your room all day studying so you can get an A on that next test. Yes, you need the A's, but colleges look at much more than grades today. They want to see students who are well-balanced in life. Kids who perform well academically, but kids who have a great high school story to tell. So build some memories and enjoy these next four years.

THRIVING FRESHMAN TIP #2

Have Fun!

High school has the potential to be the best four years of your life. Most students will remember these four years, and remember them fondly.

High school will create powerful life experiences. Experiences that you will relive with friends the rest of your life. Many people meet their future spouse in high school. And high school, more than any other time in your life, will present opportunities to achieve. If you are into sports then you already know that every weekend is an opportunity to win a game or a match or a competition.

Every weekend is a party. Every weekend there is a big sporting event like a football game or basketball game. In the words of Ferris Beuller, **"Life moves pretty fast. If you don't stop and look around once in a while, you could miss it."**

Your ability to have fun (also known as freedom) will be a direct result of your ability to manage the activities which compete for your time. Sometimes, you are going to want to just "hang" with friends. No agenda. No goal. No party. No game. You just want to hang out and chill. We say...do it! It is critical that you have that down time to share your concerns and dreams with people who care about you. It is also important to listen to what your pals are going through as well.

The kids who really thrive in high school are the ones who can balance the heavy academic loads with their social and extracurricular activities. These students, you will find as we did, are incredibly well informed about the expectations of their instructors as well as the requirements of their dream college. And their informed minds are the result of their own investigations and not of friends or campus rumors.

Chapter 2

He Said, She Said!

We predict you will learn one of the most important lessons about high school within the first 90 days. That lesson is that most teachers don't really care if you somehow got bad information about what was expected on an assignment or what information was going to be covered on a test.

It is going to be your lazy decision to rely upon someone other than the instructor for critical information that will impact your class grade. And when that grade arrives, you will have no one to blame but yourself.

The reason we know this is going to happen is because it happened to us and the lessons were expensive. Here again, you can benefit from our experience.

THRIVING FRESHMAN TIP #3

Take Responsibility For Obtaining Correct Academic Information. Do Not Rely On Your Well-Meaning Friends.

You need to know the truth and it is critical that you do some basic investigation work for yourself. The fact that you are reading this book is a great start, but it's an absolute truth that most of the students who feel compelled to give you advice about how to prepare for getting into college are misguided. You wouldn't trust a first year medical student to repair a torn ACL, would you? So why would you trust your fellow high school students for advice on your future?

Look, your friends—like our friends—are great. They think they are helping you and others out by sharing their beliefs about a whole host of high school issues. The problem is, more often than not they provide you with bad, or at least misunderstood, information.

We made a commitment not to lecture and we will do our best to maintain that throughout this book and through the entire series. But we need to talk student-to-student right now about personal responsibility. This is important.

The world, as we see it, is more and more becoming a place where individuals with incredible talents and potential are being drawn into a life of mediocrity. This is because of dangerous and frankly stupid social policies that are meant to create a massive population of dependent voters who will be so thankful for the free food stamps that they keep those political leaders in office. This happens when people stop accepting responsibility for their own lives and make others responsible for their happiness and even their survival. They lose inspiration and they fail to take the initiative to improve their life. Well, we reject that life. We want to encourage you to reject it as well. Never allow anyone else (not a parent, not a government, not a boyfriend or a girlfriend) put a limit on your success.

You will never get into your dream college or achieve that life you dream if you rely on others to get it for you or give it to you. This is your life and it can be exceptional because within you is the amazing power of self-motivation and self-determination.

You may struggle on a test or a homework assignment. Rather than succumbing to the desire to blame the teacher, you need to find the courage to accept responsibility. If you allow yourself to think that the problem is the teacher then you will never understand how to improve your grade. However, as soon as you acknowledge that you are responsible for your grades (and basically any result of your high school experience) the sooner you will free yourself to become the superstar you were meant to be.

By the way, you are also responsible for the sources you choose to use for other information as well. Did you get the wrong time to meet a study group? That's your fault. Did you get the wrong date for that SAT class? Nobody to blame but you. Did you drop a class because someone told you the teacher was a tool? Did the person who gave you that piece of information even have that instructor?

THRIVING FRESHMAN TIP #4

Form Your Own Opinion About Teachers!

You are going to hear a lot of student opinions about teachers. It is kind of sad that some teachers have rumors spread from students who never even took a class from that instructor. In our opinion, these mean teachers can sometimes be great advocates for the students who respond well to their teaching style. But whatever you do, you ignore your teacher at your own peril.

You see, students aren't the only people in the school you need to get to know. Getting to know your teachers will be very beneficial in many ways.

We know what you're thinking. You can't imagine ever building relationships with high school teachers because you've heard high school teachers are so much stricter than your middle school teachers or they are mean or they are weird... even creepy (by the way, those rumors were true at our schools as well.)

It is all just more high school lore. Think about it this way. Do you have some people in your life who don't like you? Why? You're a nice guy or girl. You have lots of people who like you. How come there are some who don't. Chances are they don't really know you. Maybe they heard something about you that formed a wrong opinion.

It may be true that you have some mean teachers. They may be strict, they may be weird, and they may be creepy. On the other hand, maybe you just heard that and believed it. The fact is you want your instructors to know you and like you. They can help with your grades as well as future letters of recommendation. But you need to make all the effort. This is their world and you are just living in it until you graduate.

You can and will build relationships with your high school teachers, but the type of relationship can often depend on how you start the year. And because much like teachers' reputations (good teacher or bad, strict teacher or easy) spread across a community, the reputation you develop during the first weeks of ninth grade can follow you through the next four years. It is inevitable that not every interaction with an adult will go perfectly. Again, you have the responsibility to make things right… not them.

Chapter 3

Be Smarter than the Problem!

As you start to read this next section you might start rolling your eyes. Don't! The last thing we want to do is lose you because you think we are selling out to the authority of adults. We aren't. Give us a little credit for being smarter than that.

The truth of the matter is that there are a lot of "adults" in our collective lives who are stubborn; think we are idiots; and simply won't give young people like you and us the opportunity to fly because they honestly believe we don't know what we are talking about. We (neither you nor us) can't change that right now. However, we are also smart enough to know that we NEED these adults on our side. It is critical that they feel you are worth their investment of time and money. Your success will be much more likely with strong advocates on your side.

All that is required by you is the ability to SUCK IT UP and to develop the maturity to see a bigger picture of your life.

THRIVING FRESHMAN TIP #5

Maintain A Positive And Respectful Relationship With Your Parents!

It can be hard to listen to your parents when they share their advice about preparing for certain specific academic activities. Maybe it's because their advice too often sounds like another lecture. Maybe it's because it seems like their high school experience was too long ago to be relevant to what you are going through. Maybe it is just a little rebellious teen attitude that is getting in the way. Whatever the reason, you need to develop the maturity to understand that your parents are always going to be your biggest fans and that they believe they are looking out for your best interests. In addition, because parents often foot a portion or all of the costs your post-high school education, it is in their best interests to help you succeed to a level that has the potential of lowering your college costs.

"(When it comes to the high school transition)…..the absolute number one thing that's different is the amount of freedom"

"Parents can help their new high-schoolers by setting up after-school routines at home to ensure homework gets done at and students stay organized"

(Pam Smiley, principal of Horizon High School in Adams 12, source link: http://co.chalkbeat.org/2013/08/23/seven-ways-to-prepare-for-the-transition-to-middle-and-high-school/#.Vc1mS_mqpm4)

It may be the case that you have the most amazing parents in the world. They respect you and give you tons of freedom to make your own choices. On the other hand, your parents may be super strict and controlling.

If you look at the big picture neither one of these scenarios will matter in ten years. In ten years, you will have graduated from your dream college and already living the incredible life you always dreamed of…or not.

In ten years, your future self may be sweeping out the back of that warehouse in the 100 degree heat and looking back to this day regretting your decision to battle with your parents every day and allowing that short-sided thinking to dramatically and negatively affect your life possibilities.

On the other hand, your future self might be relaxing on a warm beach drinking an ice-cold adult beverage thankfully looking back at the superhero-like freshman who had the maturity to see a bigger picture when it came to maintaining a positive relationship with your parents.

The bottom line is you need to keep your attitude in check. Thriving in high school is hard and stressful enough. Fighting with your parents all the time will make this even harder. Our advice to you is to keep your eye on the prize. Find the strength and discipline to put your differences aside and work together towards a common goal. Let us clarify this even further. YOU need to put YOUR differences aside. If YOU expect YOUR parents to put their differences aside...well kid, get used to a life of disappointment! The prize YOU need to keep YOUR eye on is for YOU. You will be the winner of the prize so it kind of makes sense that you will need to have the strength and discipline toyou're your differences aside.

High school life will be much easier with your parents on your side. We have never met a truly thriving high school student who had a horrible home life. The kids who thrive maintain very positive and strong relationships with their parents. Not surprisingly, thriving high school kids also have great relationships with their teachers as well.

THRIVING FRESHMAN TIP #6

Respect Your Teachers!

Let's say you have a legitimate beef with an instructor. You have a choice to make. You can go to war or simply swallow your pride and get through the class. Our advice is to avoid war at all times. This may be sounding like we are asking you to make all the sacrifices, right? RIGHT!! Remember, the prize for winning is an incredible future life full of possibilities. Failure to win the prize is a life of mediocrity. We are not asking you to do anything we didn't have to do. We had the horribly unreasonable teachers as well. We had to find a way through the class like you will certainly have to do. So, even though you may go home and want to scream into your pillow at how unfair the world is you will need to overcome the challenge of working with teachers you find crazy, unfair and unreasonable. Focus on your future life, not the present. You will find this simple strategy to a powerful coping skill.

Remember this is their class. This is their expertise. You may discover that you once in a great while you knew something that a teacher didn't know but that does not make you smarter. In a battle between you and the teacher you will ALWAYS lose. So be smarter than the problem.

It's easy. **The most basic things you need to do to build positive relationships with your teachers is coming to class on time and be prepared.** If you've had homework assigned, have that work prepared and turn it in on time. If you don't, you create additional hassles for teachers because if they've already graded that class assignment, they have to take time out to grade yours separately and then record your grade. And they have to be sure not to misplace your lately submitted work. One thing teachers don't need is an additional hassle. By being prompt and prepared, you won't be grouped with students who create hassles, and that's a good first step in creating a positive relationship with even the strictest teacher.

Assuming you can get your butt in class on time every day and turn in your assignments on time the next thing you need to do is actually demonstrating a commitment to the course.

Many of your classes will be graded using subjective methods from your instructor. Anyone who tells you that a teacher will not provide any level of favorability is simply wrong. However, anyone who thinks they will get the benefit of the doubt from an instructor they don't know well is also wrong. You have to understand that most teachers love what they do. They want their students to succeed.

On the other hand, teachers form opinions of students very quickly. The kids who are always late or disrupting the class are really stacking the deck against themselves.

I made it a point to visit every one of my teachers outside of class. If a teacher offered a lunch study session or test-prep session before an upcoming test, I went. If a teacher told a story about their life I would always make a positive comment. If a teacher missed a day of school, I would always send a quick email wishing them well.

Because I allowed my grades to suffer early in my high school career, I knew I had to take advantage of every opportunity to improve my academic performance. There is no way for me to know this, but it is my profound belief that I was the beneficiary of more than a few rounding errors. If I had an 89.2% in a class, but I had a great relationship with the teacher, I think that 89% became a 90% during the final grade reporting.

My advice to you is to put in an effort to get to know and support your teachers whenever you can. I did it every week and it helped. Two of my teachers wrote me personal letters of recommendation, which were critical to my college acceptance. Trust me, the time you invest in getting to know your teachers will be well worth it in the long run.

Another thing you can do is simply be respectful to your teachers. If they aren't busy as you enter the classroom, speak to them. A simple "How are you today?" goes a long way in relationship building. If during class you have a question about the lesson or an assignment, ask it at the appropriate time. If it's not related to the current topic, if it's an individual problem or concern, wait to ask the question. The best time to ask those sorts of questions is before or after class, not during instructional time.

We absolutely want to encourage you to assert yourself when you have an issue or concern. Just do it respectfully.

You've probably had the experience of watching a classmate get into a major disagreement with a teacher or administration over a minor problem. It may surprise you to know that teachers spend a massive amount of extra time dealing with disruptive and challenging students. Most teachers go to seminars and workshops to learn how to better manage their classroom. Most teachers have to stay after school many days to have meetings with students and their parents to deal with class-behavior problems. One of the most stressful parts of a teachers day is having to endure rude, inconsiderate and totally disrespectful students. This part of a teachers job must really suck. Think how you would feel if your had to stay after work one or twice a week (or more) because your boss wanted to talk to you about problems that keep happening on your job that you have almost no control to fix.

Here is what we think. We think that disruptive students in the classroom become disruptive factors in a teachers home life. They probably share with their spouses the stories of the rude kid or the one who is smart but never does his/her homework. Do you really want to be the kid that your teacher is talking about outside of school? To keep you from being that student you should concern, follow some simple steps.

First, if you're feeling stressed about something and need to talk to your teacher or an administrator about what's bothering you, the best way to begin the conversation is calmly. So breathe for a minute or two, just to calm down. Think carefully about what happened and what you want to be different. Also, ask yourself how you would like the person you will be speaking with to receive your message. You want them to believe you. You want them to understand you. You want them to know you respect them. You want them to walk away thinking, "Wow, Amanda really handled that well. That was impressive."

Once you get those things clear in your mind, approach the person. Then clearly and slowly talk with that person. Try to do it when there aren't others around, and try very hard to listen to what the other person says. Then thank him or her for taking time to speak with you, and don't expect immediate results because it is likely they are processing your concern for the first time.

Do you think it's important to learn to speak effectively to others? Sure it is. You'll find it a valuable skill, not just in high school, but throughout your adult life. Many times there will be things you don't understand or you don't agree with, and the best thing to do is to speak with someone about them. It's the only way you have a chance of getting what you want. How else will people know what's bothering you unless you tell them? You just need to remember to express things in a respectful manner when things aren't going your way.

Try to remember that teachers are in fact part of the human race and not aliens or robots. They feel emotions just like you. Your kindness is likely to be repaid with kindness. Remember the title of this section is called "What Good Can Come Of This? What Bad Can Come Of This?". If you can manage to express your views in a kind and respectful way the worst thing you will probably experience is some returned kindness. The best thing that could happen is your concern is addressed quickly and resolved exactly the way you had hoped.

A common issue that comes up concerns subjective grading. You write an essay and get a grade that is lower than what you expected. If you feel that you have been judged unfairly you have an obligation to yourself to address the situation with your teacher. Before you do, however, you need to stop and think about the words, the tone and the timing of your conversation. Remember...BE SMARTER THAN THE PROBLEM. What are the chances your gripe is going to be received in a positive way if you storm up to the teachers desk all pissed off? What are the chances that your teachers is going to bump up your grade if you say, "You are a totally unfair teacher and I demand a higher grade"? What are the chances that the teacher will even hear what you are saying if you approach her right after she had to discipline some other student? Be patient, calm and kind and you will find your teacher and the rest of the world seems quite a bit more fair than you originally thought.

THRIVING FRESHMAN TIP #8

Understand That Every Teacher Is Different!

Keep in mind that your teachers were here before you and they will be there long after you graduate. Don't make enemies. The best thing you can do for yourself is to understand the style of each teacher.

The first days of school, most teachers appear very organized even if they're really not. You can look around the classroom for clues to the ones who really aren't. For instance, are there framed posters hung evenly around the room? Are there neatly stacked papers on the teacher's desk and books arranged alphabetically or by size? Does something meaningful begin even before the tardy bell has stopped? Then chances are you're in the classroom of a super-organized educator, one who grades assignments quickly and will be sure the class finishes the syllabus by the end of the year. Lucky you!

The secret to winning with these teachers is following instructions exactly how they are written. Our experience is that these teachers can be very rough on you if you miss an assignment or turn one in late. They are rule-based instructors. Just follow the rules. Pay very close attention to directions. Keep every piece of paper these teachers hand out because they didn't give it to you to make paper airplanes.

These teachers spend a lot of time preparing their lessons and any work they give to you that was prepared in their own hand is probably going to be on your mid-terms or finals. Treat it like gold-leafed paper. In the end, these instructors teach classes that are the easiest ones for over-performing. You just need to do the work. If you just follow what this teacher says and do what's required, you'll end the end in good shape.

However, pictures torn from magazines and randomly scotch taped around the room or tattered border print on a bulletin board displaying last year's football schedule are signs of a teacher who at best thinks the appearance of a classroom doesn't matter. If you also see haphazard stacks of brittle, yellowing worksheets, changes are this teacher is not organized. These instructors require a whole different approach if you are going to thrive in their class.

Our experience is that these teachers use a lot of subjective grading methods. If you are the shy kid who sits in the back you are going to hate these teachers. Their lack of organization can be costly if you don't pay extra special attention to the course requirements. You will need to continually confirm anything that you feel is not crystal clear. You should make a point to visit this teacher during lunchtime at least a few times each semester.

The good news is that the better your relationship with these teachers, the more likely it is that you will do well. Talk to them often. Ask questions about what will be on the test. We have found that these teachers tend to be more open about their testing methods. Follow this advice and you will do well.

We know that it kind of stinks that you have to work so hard to just understand the differences between all of your teachers. Someday, all instruction may be online and that problem will be solved. For now, it just is what it is and as we said before, "You need to be smarter than the problem".

THRIVING FRESHMAN TIP #9

Send thank you letters to your teachers at the end of every semester!

Sure, you may have hated a class or two. Get over it. Life is way more enjoyable when you focus on lifting people up rather than tearing them down.

Beyond just helping you academically, it is very possible that your teachers can help you beyond high school. It is to your benefit to build strong positive relationships with your teachers. They will be asked about you and your performance in class. Your parents will ask them. Other teachers will ask them. Counselors and administrators will ask them. Even college recruiters or admission committees may ask them to give recommendations about you. Give your teachers something positive to say.

When the semester is over, sit down and HAND WRITE a very short thank you letter to each one of your teachers. They aren't robots, but they are often treated that way. Your goal is to get into a dream college right? Well standing out is the ONLY way to realize that dream. If you truly want to thrive you need to take the extra steps. It is an absolute guarantee that your teachers will remember the kind notes you send. How many kids do you think did it? Can you say..."almost none." Believe us, they will remember that thoughtful and positive gesture and it just may pay dividends down the road.

Chapter 4

Get Comfortable and Buckle Up!

There is a ton of research that demonstrates that people perform tasks at a much higher level when they are in comfortable and familiar environments. Well, we didn't really need that research to tell us something we already know intuitively.

One of the worst things about the freshman year is the challenge of just trying to figure out where you fit in. High school has a rhythm. The class schedules, the student traffic patterns, and even the social clicks are elements that can take some time to figure out. You will quickly figure out the timing needed to get from one side of the campus to the other. As you travel between classes you will pass the same faces every day. Knowing where certain groups of kids always hang out will be helpful as well.

However, you are feeling about your first year of high school you need to know that there are lots of kids feeling the same way. Some anxiety surrounding the first year of high school is normal and actually can be a little helpful as it keeps you sharp and focused. However, we want you to get comfortable with high school as quickly as possible.

We can offer a few ideas on how to accelerate the learning curve associated with becoming more comfortable at your new school but we recognize that experience and time cannot be replaced by our humble advice.

So let us offer you additional advice. Every freshman is entering this year with the same disadvantages as you. They don't know every kid in school. They don't know where all their classes are at the beginning of each semester. They aren't involved in a bunch of activities yet. They haven't made the sports teams yet, or had their positions finalized. They aren't familiar with all the songs or music that they will need to know (band or choir). They have never been in a high school play yet and they don't know the cheer or flag routines. You are all in this together and pretty much at the same point. In short, everyone is suffering from at least a bit of discomfort. You might have more or less than the next kid, but it is an absolute fact that every kid that has come before you has had to live through the freshman year. Our advice is to jump in head first.

The quicker you become comfortable with your high school, the quicker you will start to thrive.

THRIVING FRESHMAN TIP #10

Do Some Recon Work In Advance!

> *Entering any new environment can be stressful and research has shown that the more familiar you are with the environment, the more comfortable you will be ("7 tips to help teens successfully transition to high school | Fox News".)*

It is a terrible feeling to be lost in your own high school. We can't tell you how many times we each heard, "Do you know where classroom B307 is?" or "Excuse me, can you help me find the lab room for biology?" Most kids will help you but the additional anxiety you feel can have a negative impact on how you cope with your new school emotionally. Just because you can't find your class doesn't mean high school sucks. However, some people do connect the two. You really want to try to feel comfortable moving around the school quickly and efficiently.

So, take advantage of any opportunity to be in your new school. Get familiar with the building. Take time to walk through the halls; once you know your schedule, locate each classroom and "walk" through your day.

We always marveled at how our classes were scheduled. It seems like some practical joker puts these things together. You'll have a class at 9 a.m. located in a room on the far north side of the school. The class will get out at 9:55 a.m. and you will have 5 minutes to travel to the most remote classroom on the southern side of the school. Are they kidding?

Somehow, though you will figure it out just like every other kid before you. Just take it one day at a time.

High school administrators already know that the freshman year is an awkward year. As a result, they have put together some programs that are specifically aimed at helping to reduce student anxiety.

THRIVING FRESHMAN TIP #11

Go To The New Student Orientation Meetings!

Be sure to attend any orientation meetings your high school schedules. Most high schools have separate meetings for each class. Find out when your freshman orientation meeting is scheduled and go! During the meeting, you'll get a general overview of the school's layout and the types of courses offered.. It's a good opportunity to ask any questions you have and to meet with the administration, guidance counselors, and maybe even with some of your teachers. The teachers are always a bit nervous as well because they don't know what kind of students they will be getting. Introduce yourself with confidence and tell them how much you are looking forward to their class and the new school year. Teachers get excited when students get excited. Your goal is to make sure you make an impression as a smart and friendly face that your instructors will want to remember.

Meeting with the educators and administrators who run the school can have huge benefits for you. You'll begin building relationships with them (let's face it, these people will control a large part of the next four years of your life) and you may find you have an instant rapport with one or more of them. And that's a huge plus because one of the marks of a successful high school experience is having a good, caring mentor. You may find that many of these new friendly people will start throwing out words that you have never heard before. High school, as you will soon find, has a language all its own.

THRIVING FRESHMAN TIP #12

Learn The Academic Language Of High School!

One thing that will help you navigate those first few weeks will be if you learn the lingo. You'll hear all kinds of words and acronyms tossed around soon: ACT, SAT, CTE, IB, AP, and so many more. (Sounds like a bad version of a rap song?) Take a minute and look over the following list of terms. The more familiar you are with them, the more quickly you'll be able to understand what's being said during important, upcoming, high school meetings.

| ACT | The American College Test may be an entrance requirement for colleges |
| AG | Academically Gifted services |

AP course	*Advanced Placement course taught on a college level, usually a year long. The grade you receive at the end of the course will count toward high school graduation. The grade you receive on the national AP exam will determine whether or not you also receive college credit for the course*
Block Classes	*Class periods lasting 90 minutes*
Course	*Specific classes you take and pass to be eligible to graduate from high school*
Credit Unit	*Numeric value of each course you pass. Be sure you know what each is worth*
CATE or CTE	*Career and Technical Education courses are taken based on student interest, not usually as a graduation requirement*
Extracurricular	*Activities which meet outside of class time and be beneficial on your transcript*
GPA	*Grade Point Average based on the grade you've made on the courses you've taken*

Honors Course	*Challenging course meant for motivated students*
IB or IBP	*International Baccalaureate rigorous program with courses similar to AP*
Paideia	*Program encouraging students to think about more than just one subject*
Pathway	*Group of courses in just one area (see CATE)*
Quality Point	*Value given to each letter when computing the GPA*
Required course	*One you must pass to graduate*
SAT	*Scholastic Aptitude Test may be an entrance requirement for college*
SAT II	*Subject tests within the SAT which may also be entrance requirements*
Standard course	*General course which usually carries the least quality points*

| Transcript | Report of your grades, attendance, and GPA (may also include your immunizations and demographical information) |

Knowing the lingo will do more than just help you understand the ideas behind what the administrators, counselors, and teachers are saying because understanding those ideas will help you develop your plan for a successful freshman year.

So as you are learning the school geography and academic language you will want to look good as well. This may or may not be a big issue with you or at your school. We live in Southern California so its pretty simple here. Everybody wears shorts and flip flops to school. Style and brand loyalty is not very significant (thank goodness). But we do know that in some parts of the country and world, this can be a major issue. We can't change the trends and fads but maybe we can help you think a little differently about the clothes you wear.

THRIVING FRESHMAN TIP #13

Style Isn't A Label!

We debated about even mentioning this, but there are a lot of people out there who struggle with this.

There are tons of YouTube videos that give advice about what to wear every day. We read a blog that actually said certain colors will help you succeed in life. Really? C'mon, just be who you are.

We can tell you with great certainty that the secret to a great high school experience begins with you being authentic. Your friendships will be deeper and more meaningful. What you wear matters more to you than to your friends. But, we also recognize that confidence is deeply impacted by how you look and feel every day.

Look, high school is a great place to learn a lot of general and some specific knowledge. But equally important is the fact that you will learn a lot about yourself. The research we've read is consistent with our experiences. Specifically, students often dress a certain way to mask personality or behaviors that they wish to change.

We don't want to sound like psychologists because we are anything but that. However, if you would allow us to provide a humble and friendly piece of advice... focus on your behavior and insecurities and worry less about your clothes. High school is a great place to reinvent yourself because there are so many kids, groups, cliques, and activities that you can pretty much find support for whoever or whatever you want to be.

It may be true that you want to change something about yourself. If you've been a procrastinator, you may want to change that. You may want to overcome being painfully shy or bossy, but drastically changing your appearance without working on your behavior will not give you any meaningful results.

Maybe you want to stop being bossy. Start with the people in your house. Practice on your family by treating them in kind ways. Instead of telling your younger sister, "Get away from me," say, "I need some space right now, can we do this later?" Changing the type of shoe you wear won't make you a kinder person; practicing kindness is what will make you kinder.

Maybe you want to overcome shyness. You can begin practicing now. When you meet people you don't know this summer, even if you will only see them for a short time, be the first one to speak by simply saying, "Hello, how are you today?" And as hard as it might seem, look them in the eye when you say it. New hairstyles won't make you a more outgoing person. Practicing ways to become more comfortable speaking with people will help you overcome shyness.

Procrastination a problem? Changing the type of shirt you wear won't help you complete tasks. Developing—and making yourself stick to—a schedule will.

Are there any good, practical suggestions about what to wear the first day of ninth grade? Actually, it is pretty simple-

- **Shower every day (sounds lame right but you would be surprised how many kids just roll out of bed and head off to school without showereing. In about 4 hours, the body starts to release those odors that...well, the odors that the rest of us would prefer to not have to deal with before lunch).**
- **Smile a lot and be fully present when people are talking to you**

Whatever you wear needs to be fit your school's dress code and fit you well. Be sure you understand and follow the dress code, or you may find that first day outfit some article called "*mega cool*" causes you to be called out on dress code violations. That's not the kind of attention you want on your first day.

CHADNEY'S NOTES

Look, I get it, looking like a million dollars is freaking awesome! Your Snapchats are on point, your Instagrams are fly as hell, and your style is fresh! But at the end of the day people really do not care that much what you wear. Just wear something you feel comfortable in. If you feel comfortable in fly clothes, then were those. But if you were like me and just love sweats; well then, wear those instead of those "fly clothes". Your real friends will not care what you wear and if they do... they are not your real friends.

Be comfortable with who you are! And know that whether your style is hipster, gangster, athletic, or country, your style is what you feel most comfortable with.

So, wear what YOU want to wear. Don't
wear what others think you should wear.

Wear comfortable clothes; remember you'll be sitting in those awkward school desks a long time. Also, this isn't the day to break in new shoes; try to do that on weekends because poor fitting shoes can ruin your whole day. You don't want or need anything to distract you from what's happening in class.

We know this sounds crazy to even mention this stuff and chances are you would figure this all out for yourself, but that is not what this book is about. We want you to thrive. Why should you spend time worrying about clothes when you need to focus on grades? Why should you spend one day experiencing blisters because your new shoes didn't fit right? If you want to get blisters on the weekend... no problem. But our goal is to try to help you avoid going through these stupid plights. They are unnecessary and absolutely do not need to be part of a thriving freshman's high school experience.

Another part of high school that can create discomfort... especially for freshman is lunchtime. For many kids, eating or sitting alone can be an emotionally traumatic experience.

Some freshman are very self-conscious about this, which is ironic because we guarantee you that there will be many days ahead when you just want to sit alone and cram for that test in the next class period.

However, we recognize that lunchtime is a special event that should be addressed.

THRIVING FRESHMAN TIP #14

Plan Your Lunchtime Meets In Advance!

Cafeteria time is by far the one time during the school day that causes nightmares, both for the students as well as the adults in the building. It's a time when large numbers of people need to move through lines in a short amount of time and then be contained in a small space, which is a nightmare for the administrators. It's a time when large quantities of a variety of healthy, nutritious food, both hot and cold, need to be prepared and served quickly, which is a nightmare for the cafeteria staff. And it's often the largest block of time (aside from before or after school) when students have the opportunity to socialize. You wouldn't think to be able to talk with others would cause nightmares for students, but it does.

If you have friends around you, take the opportunity to catch-up. If you don't, take the time to talk to new people. Most schools are so big nobody knows everyone, and so your offer of conversation will be welcomed.

However, often times kids are sitting in small groups and it is pretty unlikely that you will feel comfortable walking up and joining that group. Here are a couple of tips that can help:

1. **Pre-arrange a lunch meeting place with anyone you might already know. Don't wait until lunchtime to try to find a friendly face. You will be wondering around feeling very uncomfortable and lonely. Set up a lunch meet the day before or early in the morning.**

2. **Don't eat the school food if you can avoid it. The lines are too long it cuts into your free time way too much. Lunch is a great time to recharge your**

batteries and just relax so come prepared with your own food. Besides, most of the lunch food served today is terrible because of a politicians who want to take away our freedom to eat the food we want to eat (sorry- sometimes we can't help ourselves).

Whatever you do during lunch, be sure to do these two things: eat and relax. Research has shown lunch times, and the socialization that occurs during lunch, are beneficial for students. Those 20-30 minutes give your body the nutrition it needs and your mind the break it needs before continuing the rest of the day. And your body and mind will need replenishing because, depending on your schedule, you can have 3-5 classes left after lunch. So, eat well, talk with people, and breathe. Just think, the hardest part of your first day is over.

We can't finish this chapter on getting comfortable without addressing one of the single biggest causes of discomfort. Bullying, sadly, is a reality at every school. Our opinions on this matter are strong and we don't pull punches. When it comes to bullying you are either part of the problem or you are part of the solution.

THRIVING FRESHMAN TIP #15

Report Acts of Intimidation Immediately!

According to almost all research statistics we could find, bullying is increasing. However, there is no evidence of any school condoning bullying. In fact, all but one state, Montana, have laws against bullying, although the strength of those laws varies from state to state. (BullyPolice.org)

So, how can you prepare for the reality of bullying? Many schools have either developed or adopted an anti-bullying program. Find out if your school has one. Find out how it works. You also need to decide how you are going to deal with bullying personally.

If you end up being bullied or you witness someone being bullied, you may have a fear that if you report it the bullying will get worse or be directed at you. This is a tough decision and it sucks that you or frankly, anyone has to face this dilemma.

Everyone not directly involved in the situation will tell you to report the incidents. Allow us to jump on that bandwagon. Report it! The stress, the danger, and the overall impact on your high school experience will be incredibly negative if you let the bullying continue.

Why do kids bully? We have no idea. They're punks and every one of them should be expelled and do time in juvenile hall for intimidating other people. But that doesn't help you today.

Today you need to make a decision about your character. We want you to encourage you to establish a principle for the way you will live and behave during your high school years.

CHADNEY'S NOTES

I can remember walking to class one day and getting literally knocked to the ground by the high school quarterback who just looked and laughed at me. The guy was surrounded by four of his fellow Neanderthal football players. I couldn't exactly do anything at the time, but I do remember other kids just walking by and leaving me to my own defense. The incident passed quickly, but it left an impression on me. I made a decision at that point to never be the guy who just walked by.

Don't get me wrong. I was not looking for trouble. However, anytime I saw a kid being pushed around or being made fun of by other kids— sometimes my friends—I did something about it. Sometimes this meant stepping in which I only did when I knew the situation would not escalate. Sometimes I reported it to a teacher or administrator and sometimes I just got in my friends face and told them to knock it off. You need to make your own judgment calls about what to do because every situation is different. All I can tell you is that I feel very strongly about the subject and believe every student deserves to have an awesome high school experience without being tortured by classmates.

Bullying is perhaps the worst possible thing you may experience in high school. If you are in a position to help other kids who are being bullied you should help. To the bullied kid, you will be like a cape-donning superhero (Super-Freshman.)

Seriously, bullies have no idea how their thoughtless actions torture and torment their victims. A lot of these troglodytes simply think they are goofing around or "having a little harmless fun." The fact is, that it is neither harmless nor fun.

Inserting yourself into the situation by reporting the event, you will most likely forever change the life of the bullied student. High school administrators will absolutely protect your identity. They just need to be informed of the situation so they can do something about it.

While the plots in movies and television shows might present students harassing others as inevitable or even comical, it's neither. Anyone who has ever been bullied knows this. So figure out right now what the future you is going to be like and make a commitment to those principles. Character is demonstrated through active decision-making and you are now presented with your first high school character decision.

Before we complete this section on getting comfortable, we need to address another part of high school that can often result in anxiety for new students. Lunchtime at every high school moves at a pretty frenetic pace and for students who don't know many other students, it can suck...especially if you eat alone.

Chapter 5

P=MV (Momentum= Mass x Velocity)

Beginning this year, every grade, every award, and every activity will either build a bridge or become a stumbling block in your journey toward college acceptance. Beginning this year, your steps can also move you toward or away from avenues for funding your college ambitions. So, yeah, freshman year is a pretty big deal, and you need to make the most of it.

In fact, research has shown that your level of success during your freshman year can be a determining factor in your success in high school (Willens). It's even a factor in determining whether you move on to college or drop out of high school.

According to an article published by McCallumore and Sparapani in Education Digest, ninth graders have a pattern of more missed school days and more misbehavior referrals than any other grade ("UChicago Consortium on Chicago School Research.").

One of the most chilling statistics is that 22% of ninth grade students have to repeat their freshman year ("The First Year of High School: A Quick Stats Fact Sheet").

Even more alarming is knowing that researchers Allensworth and Easton found students with more than one semester "F" in core subjects at the end of the year, coupled with fewer than five full course credits, are not just less likely to attend college but are more likely not to graduate high school (Allensworth and Easton, 2005).

According to yet another report, it's not just your freshman year but the first 30 days of your freshman year that are the most important because your attendance during the first 30 days of your freshman year can be an even stronger indication of your success in high school than the grades you make (Jerald, 2006).

Some researchers believe that once they know about your performance in ninth grade, anything else they discover about you would do little to change their prediction on whether or not you'll graduate high school (10).

But don't think to fail or not attending are the only worries during your ninth grade. According to The Consortium on Chicago School Research at the University of Chicago, freshmen *with less than a C average* are more likely to drop out than graduate (11). That means if you slip during the first semester or two of high school, it will be difficult to recover enough to participate in graduation ceremonies with your classmates.

So if poor performance is an indication of future success than it stands to reason that students who perform well will continue to perform well if they just follow the same methods all the time. Well, we agree and we think this is really one the big secrets to thriving in high school.

Specifically, find out what is working and keep doing it.

THRIVING FRESHMAN TIP #16

Build Momentum Every Day!

Everything you've done prior to entering high school has been merely preparation. Perhaps a better way of putting it is that you have been building momentum (remember our word problems?). You have built up a head of steam intellectually, physically, and emotionally and it is set to carry you into and through these next four years…the best years of your life.

It is critical that you understand that every day of high school represents opportunities to increase your momentum or to engage in negative experiences that can slow you down.

Business track the number of days without employee injuries. Football teams track the number of consecutive wins. Reformed alcoholics track the number of days without a drink. You need to track and measure your performance like this as well.

When you answer roll for the first class on the first day on your freshman year, you begin compiling a permanent attendance record. This record will follow you and could have an impact on your college opportunities.

Your grade on the first assignment you submit—whether it's a homework assignment or a major test—begins the permanent record of your GRADE POINT AVERAGE, and it will also follow you and impact your college opportunities. These items, in combination with many other elements of your high school career, will make up a document that college admission officers will look at to determine your fit for their college. This document is called your TRANSCRIPT.

What's on a transcript? Your transcript will list all the classes you take during your high school years, your attendance record, certain disciplinary events, your class rank, some demographic information and of course the grades you received in each class (the freshman year will be a part of that transcript.) Those grades will be averaged into your grade point average. While college applications vary from college to college, all colleges will ask for your transcript as part of your application, and most colleges place considerable value on your grade point average (GPA.) Colleges feel grades are a good indication of not only the knowledge you've gained about the material covered but also if the habits and strategies you possess will lead to your success in college-level work.

THRIVING FRESHMAN TIP #17

Obsess About Your Grades!

This is kind of a no-brainer right? You know you need good grades to get into that dream college. However, we don't want you to just know this information…we want you to obsess about it.

The single biggest factor that you can control and that will have the greatest impact on your post-high school possibilities is your grades. Know it! Share it! Live it! Grades matter!

How can you get the best GPA possible? To start with you need to understand the scoring values. In most cases, grades such as "A" or "B" are translated into a numeric value.

A= 4

B= 3

C= 2

D= 1

F= 0

Note: Pass/Fail classes do not typically counted towards your GPA. You do get credit for the class, but no points are added to your overall GPA.

Not all classes are weighted equally. Some, such as Honors or Advanced Placement classes, count more than others. For instance, if you make a "B" in a standard class, it's usually given a numerical value of "3"; but a "B" in an Honors or Advanced Placement class is usually given a higher numerical value, usually a "4."

So, if your school has a 4 point scale, and you make an "A" in an Honors or Advanced Placement class, the numeric value is usually bumped up to a 5. This gives you a definite edge when grades are averaged. It also explains how students can graduate with a GPA of more than 4 (some with a 5!) when their schools use a 4 point scale.

This is where you'll be able to understand why all the preparation prior to entering high school is so important. That preparation prepares you for the higher level courses which give you an edge over those who will be taking the standard classes. However, Honors and Advanced Placement classes often have pre-requisites that must be met before you enroll. You might need to have already taken a particular course or earned a specific grade in a prior course. Some high schools require written letters of recommendation from your middle school teachers before they will allow you to take honors courses as a freshman.

We will go into advanced placement classes later and how thriving students get these classes. For now, you just need to understand how the grading system works because it shows up everywhere (report cards, transcripts...even job resumes).

CHADNEY'S NOTES

My freshman year ended with four "C's". Some of you reading this book might think a C average isn't too bad. On the other hand, most of you reading this book will realize that C's don't get you into college; C's aren't on the path to an extraordinary life; and C's don't impress companies that hire students for part-time work. My inability to stay motivated and manage time and tasks was destroying my future happy life. It took a while, but I finally found my stride and was able to dramatically turn my academic picture around. Don't get me wrong, I still had to work extremely hard for my grades, but better studying techniques, time management, and scheduling tools helped me become a straight "A" student.

The thing you will figure out quickly is that one bad grade on a test can take a long time to recover from in terms of your overall class grade. It is so much easier to begin with some high test scores than the other way around.

FRESHMAN TIP #18

Start Strong! Do Every Assignment On Time And Never Miss A Class. You Must Go On The Offensive And Attack The Freshman Academics.

As you read this information you might be wondering why such a high number of students who struggle during their freshman year fail to recover during their next three years. The answer is momentum. Once a giant snowball starts rolling down a hill it is almost impossible to stop. Kids who start strong tend to continue to do well. Students who start off with poor grades tend to continue to do poorly. More importantly, the gap between achievers and under performers will continue to grow so that by the junior year the gap is insurmountable. Here is a word problem for you: Two high school students, Josh and Chad, are both traveling north on skateboards. Chad is traveling at 10 mph and Josh is traveling at 8 mph. In one hour, how much further will Chad be than Josh? The answer is 2 miles right? What if the word problem went like this:

Two high school students, Josh and Chad, are traveling on skateboards. Chad is traveling north at 10 mph and Josh is traveling south at 8 mph. In one hour, how far apart will they be? The answer 18 miles.

The point is you must start out on the right foot going in the right direction.

The inspiration for writing this book came from a potentially devastating firsthand experience. As a freshman, I was pretty much just interested in the incredible new social opportunities.

Making friends always came much easier than making great grades. But a poor grade on a test always resulted in a reassuring pat on the back from my new friends who would say, "Don't worry Chad, nobody looks at the freshman year. This is a transition year and doesn't count on your overall GPA."

It is the biggest pile of crap you will hear this year. Anyone who tells you that the freshman year is a throwaway year simply does not know what they are talking about.

You need to start strong. I didn't. During my freshman year of high school, I ended up with four "C's". That pretty much eliminated about 30% of the potential U.S.

colleges that I would have a realistic shot at attending. In addition, my opportunities to get into honors courses during my sophomore year were diminished as well.

Perhaps more importantly, I simply learned bad study habits. Sure, I made a ton of friends (friends I don't see or talk to anymore) and I attended a lot of parties and school events but little did I know how much the "freshman year doesn't matter" advice would affect my future high school career (but that is a book for another day).

The claim that the freshman year doesn't impact your college opportunities is nothing but lore spread by ignorant students. Freshman year matters a lot.

THRIVING FRESHMAN TIP #19

Strive To Be In The Top 10% Of Your Class!

Colleges give special consideration to students who are ranked in the top ten percent of their classes. This doesn't mean you have to be in the top ten, just the top ten percent. For instance, if there are 2,000 students in your class, you need to be in the top 200, and if there are 400, you need to be in the top 40 to be considered in the top ten percent. There's no question about the importance of grades in high school, and it all starts with that first grade. Grades can help you in other ways, too.

For instance, colleges often want you to submit your score on one or more standardized test such as the SAT or ACT. Different colleges require different levels of achievement on these tests. ("U.S. ACT Exam Score Average Slips, but More Students College-ready, Report Says")

Students from the North East who took the 2010 ACT scored 22.1 or higher in all four benchmarks than the national average of 21.0, and students in the Lower South and parts of the South West scored 21.0 or lower in all four benchmarks than the national average (20.pdf.)

Generally speaking, a combination of a high GPA and higher than average SAT or ACT score will assure your spot in a good four-year college. But getting a top 10% ranking in your school is almost a luck. Shoot for the sky because if you fall short you are among the stars (it's a little cheesy, but it captures the point).

Section

02

Grades Before Everything Else!
(The Great Equalizer)

Chapter 6

Getting Down To Business

Remember, the name of this book is Good Freshman to Thriving Freshman. Our goal is not to help bad students become good students. Rather, our focus is in trying to help good students become superstars. The strategies and ideas you are about to learn absolutely work. Stay with us here as we begin to reveal the path to becoming a superstar high school student.

THRIVING FRESHMAN TIP #20

Find A Study Buddy In Every Hard Class!

You will definitely have a more concentrated schedule than you might be used to once you begin high school. You'll be responsible for more schoolwork and probably more activities outside of school, too. But, don't let it stress you out. Stay organized. Plan out a schedule (we'll talk more about that later,) and don't just post it on a wall somewhere. Stick to your schedule.

Our best advice to you is to attack the workload rather than to let it attack you. By this we mean you need to go on the offensive. Don't ever let yourself be surprised by upcoming projects, homework assignments, or important tests. And never ever allow yourself to get behind. Catching up never works out like you think it will in your head. Typically, you keep getting the same results.

One great way to stay on top of your studies is to find a fellow classmate and become study partners. In college, just about every student has a study partner or group that meets before big tests. Regrettably, neither one of us knew this strategy during our freshman year, but thriving freshman know about it and they do it.

Michael Loui, Professor of Electrical and Computer Engineering and a University Distinguished Teacher-Scholar at the University of Illinois, studied the impact on grades for students who attend small study groups. He found that students who attend at least six study groups during the year can boost their grades by as much a one-half of a grade (5.5%). That is a huge increase and can have an enormous impact on your GPA.

As we were looking back at our report cards and final class grades from our freshman year, we discovered that almost 2/3rds of our classes ended with upper mid-range scores like 86.5% or 89.2%. Looking back, we feel like idiots for not using this strategy to help us thrive. Take advantage of this powerful study technique and find study partners or groups during the early days and weeks of school in every class. As you begin to take harder classes this strategy will come indispensable.

THRIVING FRESHMAN TIP #21

Stretch Your Capabilities Early And Often!

As a freshman, you may be very limited in terms of your ability to take honors or AP classes. Every school is different. However, if you can, try to get into as many as possible.

They are typically not harder classes, but the workload is certainly more significant. Colleges understand this and absolutely look at academic coursework when making admission decisions. Again, anyone who tells you that honors courses during the freshman year really don't count is a fool.

> "Tips for High School Freshman........If you want to compete for top-tier programs, you need to begin taking AP courses (or IB courses if you are in an International Baccalaureate program). I suggest that you take 1-2 each year and then test at the end of that year, so you don't have to cram everything into your junior and senior year. Take the most rigorous course for your abilities. While most admissions officers would like to see "As" in AP courses, getting an "A" in a non-AP course is the often the equivalent of a "B" in an AP course. These courses are sometimes limited in the freshman year, so check with your guidance counselor before you register for classes."
>
> (Natalie Grinblatt Epstein, former MBA Admissions Dean and Director at Ross, Johnson, and Carey, source link: http://blog.accepted.com/2014/06/10/getti ng-ready-to-apply-to-top-tier-colleges-and-universities-freshman-year)

Remember, you are building a resume while you are in high school. That resume will be the most important tool for helping you get into your dream college. As a freshman, you may not have any idea where you want to go to school, which is actually the best argument for really trying to push yourself early. If your future self-decides to apply to an Ivy League school you want to make sure you don't screw up that opportunity this year.

"Taking and passing an AP class and its exam proves you are capable of an intro-level college course. Many colleges will give you credit or higher class standing for passing AP scores."

(Halle Edwards, graduate from Stanford University, source link: http://blog.prepscholar.com/how-many-ap-classes-should-you-take)

Also, getting accustomed to the heavier coursework early will help you throughout your high school career. With the additional work, you may find yourself feeling a little more stressed out but the advantages of higher level classes are significant.

CHADNEY'S NOTES

I started slow and didn't take honors courses until my junior year. It wasn't until the end of my sophomore year that I decided I wanted to go a U.S. Military Academy for my college education.

As anyone will tell you, getting into one of those schools can be like trying to get into an Ivy League school. My last two years of high school were basically confined to school and soccer. I spent most of my lunches studying inside one of my teacher's classrooms. In addition, I rarely went to bed before midnight as I put in tons of extra hours to ensure my grades were as strong as they could be. In short, I missed out on a lot of the high school social activities because I started my high school career too slowly.

JOSHUA'S NOTES

I started very strong this year taking honors classes and pulling straight A's. I have learned some excellent study habits and feel very comfortable with next year's course schedule which includes two AP classes. I also play football, write books like these, and still have enough time to enjoy a reasonable social life.

I watched Chad struggle during high school. However, once the focus kicked in, he managed to find the self-discipline to do what he needed to accomplish his goal... which he did. The cost, in my opinion, was very high. He basically missed out on a lot of the high school social experiences because of his need to play catch up. So for me, I knew I wanted to start strong. So far, it's working out pretty well.

If you do find yourself becoming stressed out, talk about it with a friend, a parent, a teacher, or a counselor at school. They can help you develop strategies so that you can fulfill all your responsibilities without having a meltdown.

The fact is that a large percentage of students are not adequately prepared for the transition to high school. Those students may want to follow a different strategy. If that is you, don't be embarrassed or feel like the situation is hopeless. You are not alone.

Our parents were continually on us to get good grades and the fact is that they grounded us more than once for falling behind. Their involvement did have an impact but at the end of the day, it was our life. We learned that the courses we took, the grades we received and the activities we pursued were only going to happen if we took charge. We had to make the effort.

You need to take responsibility for your destiny and for your choices. Your future self-demands it. The honors and AP classes provide an advantage on your transcripts, your overall GPA, and your class rank. Which is why they are so heavily sought after. Some kids get in because they are just that smart. Other kids get in because they fight for the right. Our advice, fight either way.

THRIVING FRESHMAN TIP #22

Be An Advocate For Yourself!

If your intention is to compete with the elite academic students at your school you MUST be proactive and fight for admittance into the higher level courses. These spots are typically limited and we are here to tell you that the squeaky wheel gets the oil. You must advocate for yourself and pester and pursue these coveted opportunities with gusto. The evidence is clear that the more people you have helping you stay focused and on course during your college quest, the more likely it is that you will find the success that you seek. However, too many students fail to accept any responsibility for managing this journey. If we were standing in front of you we would probably act like crazy dirll instructors or high powered motivational speakers in an attempt to help you understand that you MUST find the confidence to speak up for yourself. Some things you can't control. Some things you can control. But there are many thngs that might seem out of your control until you actively and aggressively insert yourself into the situation.

JOSHUA'S NOTES

Here is a tip that can help you. Let's say you want to take an honors biology class but you know space is limited. You need to build a case. First, you need to tell the high school counselor that you or academic advisor at your school that you have wanted to be a doctor your entire life. You then need to produce letters from friends or family members who are currently in the medical profession who will unequivocally reinforce this statement. They need to write a persuasive letter that indicates how well suited you are for this field of study and any anecdotes they can add to enhance the recommendation would be very helpful.

You need to immediately find an opportunity to volunteer at a hospital, doctor's office, dental office...wherever you can. It doesn't matter what you do it just matters that you show a commitment to this field of study. I needed to get into a specific science class at my high school, but the spots were very limited. All I can tell you was that I met with the instructor and gave an impassioned plea. When I walked out of that meeting the instructor knew that as far as I was concerned, my entire future was dependent upon me getting into that class. I pulled an "A" both semesters last year.

Class assignment is based upon a small group of educators who take a very subjective view of the whole process. Get in there and fight for your classes and don't take no for an answer.

Even if you don't meet all the stated requirements in the higher-level courses, some schools will only allow you to enroll if your parents sign a waiver giving their permission. Just be sure you understand that in higher level courses, you will be expected to do work with a higher level of knowledge. Our personal experience is that AP courses or Honors courses are not harder, they just require more work. The classes move faster and cover more information but the problem solving, analysis, and writing is pretty much the same.

These classes are taught by teachers with high expectations of their students. You will need to participate in class more often demonstrating that you are keeping up with the coursework. It definitely will require a greater effort but if you want to go to an elite college, this extra effort might be well worth it.

Transcripts often list your Class Rank, which is usually based on your GPA. Class rank simply demonstrates how your GPA ranks compared to the other students in your grade. The student having the highest grade average would rank highest. For instance, if there are 100 people in your class, the person ranked #1 would have the highest GPA average, and the person ranked #100 would have the lowest GPA average. Those who are ranked in the middle (#50-60) would be considered "average."

Class rank often also determines the Valedictorian and Salutatorian for your graduating class. You know those graduation speeches that go viral? The Valedictorian and Salutatorian (#1 and #2 in class rank) are usually the ones who give speeches during the graduation ceremony.

THRIVING FRESHMAN TIP #23

Never Ever Ever Ever Ever Forget Why You're There!

You are in school to learn. It is probably not too hard for you to look around your school and identify the kids who are intellectually challenged. As a teenager, this disadvantage may not be that big of a deal because the consequences of being stupid (we are not referring to special needs kids but rather those lazy morons who think school is a big social experiment) are pretty minimal at this age. We wrote about the "student gap" earlier. Each year the gap between students who know how to use their brains and the students who refuse to use their brains grows. By the time you graduate college, less than eight years from now, that gap will be enormous.

The life trajectory of intelligent people is vertical and absolutely reflects a powerful and uniquely American culture that emphasizes personal accomplishment. Specifically speaking, smart people have no limits to their dreams of living an exceptional life. On the other hand, the idiots (again, we have no time for political correctness) of this world are destined to watch achievers with jealousy and envy. You must learn to rely upon a relentless pursuit of excellence in everything you do including the way you study. Stupid is a choice. So is greatness.

Another thing you can do to increase the success of your time in high school is to establish a rigid study routine. High school will be different from your middle school experience. There will be more distractions, more reasons to put studying off. So our advice to you is to schedule a set time, even if it is before school. Start today because your goal is to develop study habits. Habits take time to become part of a lifestyle. It is a lot harder to develop correct habits during the school year. Tom Brady didn't learn how to throw a football during games… he learned during countless hours of practice and pre-season training. All we see is the result of his training commitment. A study like Tom Brady trains.

We were taught to concentrate on a studious activity such as reading before school. We would spend at least 30 minutes every morning focused on this type of schoolwork. Another thing we would do is focus on research. We know a lot of kids who jump into their social media accounts first thing in the morning. However, if you train yourself to do research for school projects during this time you will find the homework goes much faster when you get home because the prep work is already done.

Which brings up another point. The most effective study sessions you will have will be the result of work you did prior to sitting down and cracking open the book.

"Scheduling and managing time wisely are important for all students. If you miss important appointments and deadlines you will cause complications to both your academic and social lives. This causes anxiety, frustration, guilt, and other nasty feelings."

Another suggestion is to combine several activities into one-time spot. While commuting to school, listen to taped notes. This allows up to an hour or two a day of good study review."

(Gail M. Zimmerman, Assistant Dean of First-Year Students and Academic Counselor, Dartmouth College and Bob Nelson, et al, Learning Resource Centers, Rutgers University, source link: http://www.mcpsmt.org/Page/3537)

THRIVING FRESHMAN TIP #24

Get Organized and Stay Organized!

There will be plenty of information given out the first day and the first weeks of school. You'll get a syllabus explaining the details of each class, such as how grades are averaged and which subjects will be covered. Most classes will have a list of rules to follow in addition to the rules in your student handbook. You'll get information on the supplies you'll need for a class, how to submit completed work, and what to do about missing or late work.

If your school has gone digital, create a file for each class and within each class's file create a folder for the first day's (or week's) information. If your school relies on hardcopies, have a separate section in your notebook for each class. You may even want a separate notebook for each class. A three-ring binder would be best because it allows you to add information throughout the year. We'll talk more later about how to using these files or notebooks can help lead to greater success.

Always be ready to study because if your days get hectic, you may only get a few 20 or 30-minute blocks of time. Don't spend that time looking for pens or pencils. If you get yourself organized you will be ready to go.

This also goes for your locker. Messy lockers are the classic characteristic of a high school student. However, look around some day. You will be surprised how many kids have their act together. Their books are organized by their class schedule. Their folders and notebooks are clean set up properly. They might even have a calendar posted with important academic dates or school functions marked off. Now look at your locker! C'mon, gets it together. Maybe your mom is right and you are a total slob. Well, our advice is work on fixing your slob issues at home. At school, you need to develop a zero tolerance for your personal disorganization.

Stop wasting time scouring through loose papers to find that homework assignment. Don't think this is having an impact on your school performance? Think again.

Kids with clutter lockers often don't turn in papers because they can't find them. Students who actually want to get the points on that assignment get tardy notices because they spent all that time looking for their work. Finally, and perhaps worst of all, it is possible that you will misplace a syllabus that contains a test date. Unless you commit to fixing this today, the problem will get worse because the papers in your locker just keep stacking up. You will be spending more time looking and miss more assignments. But it is totally avoidable. It takes just a small effort on your part. Here is a tip, at the end of every day ask yourself, "What would happen if my future-self came back and opened this locker?". If the answer is "kick my ass" then you have some work to do.

If you can't keep your locker tidy than try not using the locker. For our experience, Joshua just keeps everything in his 50lb back pack. At least when he gets to class he has everything with him.

THRIVING FRESHMAN TIP #25

Make a Study Plan!

Begin your freshman year with a study plan. We've already talked about the reasons making a study plan will help you, especially during your Freshman Year. Let's talk about the particulars of a successful study plan.

First, you need to find the right place ("Preparing to Study: A Good Study Place".) Because you want your place to be available when you need it, pick a little-used spot in your home. Don't have a room all to yourself? Then work with your family to develop a schedule for a time and place where you can work uninterrupted. Be sure the spot you select has a desk or table, or any flat surface large enough for you to not just write but also to spread out your materials when needed. Proper lighting is important, too, because you'll be doing a ton of reading there. Having a place to store your books and supplies is a plus. Think of it as your private nest and surround yourself with things that will make good use of your time while you're there. You will be spending a fair amount of time there.

JOSHUA'S NOTES

I have a very simple formula for getting good grades and staying on top of my grades. I come home from school after football practice, take a shower, make a snack and go straight into my studies. I have a desk in my room where I keep all my school supplies. I turn my phone off and my parents give me space to just focus on my school work. Chores get put aside until the school work is done. My only break is for dinner. There are dozens of routines you can come up with, but I think the key is dedicating time and space and then sticking to it. It only works because everyone in my family understands the study plan.

Once you have a study place, set your time schedule. As we suggested earlier, you may have already decided on a specific time and begun the habit of using it for preparing for school. Now that you've been through a day of your course schedule, you have a better idea about which time period (and how much time) will work best for you. Once you've decided on an established study time, keep it every day. And don't procrastinate starting ("10 Habits of Highly Effective Students".) It's important this time be used, and the longer you put off beginning the less likely you are to develop the studying habit you need to be successful this year. Alert friends and family not to call or text during this time, and contact them only when you have a class related reason.

If you are trying to get into the college of your dreams, you cannot procrastinate. I get it, why the heck would someone work on their studies so far in advance? After all isn't there a more important Netflix show that needs to be finished? A more important NBA game that needs to be watched? Or a more important Call of Duty level that needs to beat? The short answer is no.

I fully understand that procrastination is so much more convenient. But if you want to be a striving student in school you cannot afford to procrastinate. I will not sugarcoat this for you. It will be very hard to keep ahead of your studies. Especially when your friends, teammates, and classmates all are finishing assignments the day before they are due. But you have to have the foresight that high school is setting up your life for success. And you have to have the determination to keep working hard and staying ahead of your studies so that you can attend the school of your dreams.

THRIVING FRESHMAN TIP #26

Make A Study Schedule!

One thing you should always have with you is a study schedule, and there are many ways to develop one. Some teachers will give you a schedule (typically referred to as a syllabus) for their courses but some won't. Take any syllabus you receive and combine them. You need to see the ENTIRE study picture and not just view it class by class. Many of the thriving students we interviewed find planning a month ahead to be beneficial. Your schedule should include each class and the days of the month (or week). You then need to populate your major class assignments into this calendar. Include projects, quizzes and tests. Then, working backwards, you begin to fill in your schedule with the estimated amount of time you will need to study for each assignment or test. Our recommendation is to add 30% more time for studying your freshman year or at least until you feel like you understand the rythym of each course.

It is critical that you think long-term about your study goals. Cramming is for losers. Don't wait until the last minute because you simply will not retain information on a consistent enough basis to over perform on your academics. There is a pile of research available which clearly demonstrates that more frequent but shorter study sessions produce significantly better results.

Once you have completed your study schedule you can begin to see the holes in your schedule for other activities. We called it "me-time". This is when you work on leveling up on your favorite video games.

Prioritizing what you do with your time is a very important habit to develop during the beginning of your first year of high school. In fact, most research points to the ability to prioritize as one of the hallmarks of successful students. Other qualities that show up in research of successful students is having knowledge of requirements, a clear sense of goals, and the ability to organize and manage time ("qualities of a successful college student".) By using a study plan, you'll soon develop all those qualities.

THRIVING FRESHMAN TIP #27

Write Homework Essays As If They Are College Application Essays!

In high school, you'll find many opportunities to write essays on specific topics. It's a given that you'll be asked to write in your English classes and probably in your social studies classes and science classes, too. You may even be asked to write during a math class or two. Take advantage of all of these opportunities and write to impress your teachers. Write as if your assignment is going to be read by a college admissions officer.

Not only will you be able to fine tune your writing skills, you'll get valuable feedback from your teachers. Use the feedback to your best advantage. One of the more common complaints we heard from a huge list of college admission officers is that students don't write to the assigned topics. The ability to follow instructions is a critical element of the college application process.

More than one person told us that following instructions was not part of the acceptance process but rather a part of their rejection process. In other words, applicants don't get points for doing what is expected. However, applications are instantly rejected if the applicant drifts off topic.

The good news is, writing is a talent that can be developed. Our advice is to relish the opportunities to write lots of papers, especially opinion papers. Who knows? Maybe your writing skills will develop so well you will be inspired to write a book or two!

Remember as you begin this first year of high school: grades are important. The higher your GPA and class rank, the more likely you are to be accepted into the college of your choice. But grades shouldn't be the only thing on your mind as you begin this year.

High grades are a culmination of a lot of different strategies and techniques; focus, discipline, organization and commitment are some of the characteristics of thriving students. Maturity is another big one. You must start acting in a way that is responsible and healthy. The first stop on this journey to maturity is the way you eat.

THRIVING FRESHMAN TIP #28

Stop Eating Like A Toddler!

For goodness sake, put down the soda and Pixie Sticks and stop chewing on those M&M's all day.

Doing well in school is about immersing yourself into a smart, deliberate, and healthy high school lifestyle. We live in an enlightened world where there is just too much information about the positive benefits good nutrition has on our attitude, focus, and energy. This sounds like a lecture, but it really isn't. We just wanted to acknowledge the fact that poor nutrition can contribute to some very negative physiological realities and we want to make sure you minimize those potential negatives.

Fatigue and unusually large emotional swings are not uncommon to high school students. The stress of trying to continually perform well academically, socially, and athletically can be hard to manage. But trying to cope with these stresses on a diet of caffeine, sugar, and processed foods will make this challenge that much harder.

One piece of advice is to begin the day with some healthy food like fruit or vegetables, and a decent serving of protein. That's right; begin this day with a good breakfast. According to the American Dietetic Association, students who eat a healthy breakfast have better concentration and problem-solving skills, and so perform better in the classroom ("The Many Benefits of Breakfast".) Plus, research at Purdue University found that adding protein to your breakfast blunts your hunger the most ("The Many Benefits of Breakfast",) which can be a real benefit by keeping you from becoming "hangry" (you know, so hungry you're angry) during class.

My favorite part of the day is lunchtime. Lunch is that special thirty minutes that I actually get to chill out and eat delicious food that reenergizes me to finish out the day strong. If there has been anything I have learned from myself and friends when we don't eat, is that when someone is hungry they tend to get very grumpy. And by grumpy I mean; short-tempered, more emotional, and more exhausted.

You do not have to eat a chipotle burrito for lunch, but you should eat something. Whether that be a piece of fruit and a sandwich, or a granola bar and some yogurt. But if you are one of those people who cannot wake up an extra two minutes in the morning to make your lunch [like me] then make your lunch the night before or bring $5 to school and buy something in the lunch line.

The bottom line is just get something in your body that will give you a little bit of

energy to finish off the day. It makes a huge
difference in your personality and will make
your afternoons feel a little less long.

It doesn't matter what you eat as long as it's healthy. Sooner
or later you are going to figure out that healthy eating is a
part of the life strategy of people who are high achievers, so
why not start now? Put that childish (but delicious) Twinkie
down and grab an apple, kid!

Section

With Friends Like That, Who Needs Enemies?

(It's Not Just Who You Know. It's Who They Want To Be!)

Chapter 7

Pick Your Friends-
Don't Let Them Pick You!

High School popularity is perhaps the most talked about in a youth-specific popular culture. There are songs written about it. There are movies and T.V. shows made about it. In fact, you and most of your friends will at some point be talking about it (or at the very least you will acknowledge that there are some kids who are super popular). However, do these kids really "run" the school in terms of social acceptance? You will quickly learn that the answer is no.

The students who seem to run the school are just those who are active and who join clubs and/or volunteer for activities. Because they are involved in so many things, it stands to reason that they know more people (and more people know them) than a student who interacts with the same small group all the time.

There is no question that your freshman year...in fact, your entire high school experience will be enhanced by having an ever-expanding network of friends. The relationships you form during the beginning of your freshman year can be very beneficial. The more people (both students and adults) you know at your high school, the more comfortable you'll feel while you're there.

You may be lucky. You may have a group of friends from middle school who will be following you to your new school. You may also already know a few of the teachers or administrators. But there will still be many you don't know. Even more important, there will be many who don't know you—YET.

However—and this may be one of the most important lessons that you can learn from this book—that is why you need to choose your friends. **Do not let people choose you as a friend.** What we mean is that too often kids find themselves in an unfamiliar or awkward place, and to deal with the discomfort they latch on to anyone who acknowledges them. This is a dangerous but understandable human condition.

Students feel a loyalty to those friendly people who "saved" them from that lonely discomfort. The problem is that the loyalty may be directed at a total loser (sorry, we have no interest in being politically correct). If you find yourself suddenly surrounded by friends who don't study or party just a little too hard, it is time to think about finding some new friends.

"Choose the right friends. Your time at high school can either be some of the best years of your life or the worst depending on who you choose to spend them with. Don't restrict yourself to one group of friends. High school presents you with the perfect opportunity to break norms and join different social circles. Your classes will be populated with people of different grades, and, contrary to popular belief, most upperclassmen are friendly and willing to help you out. Be sure to maintain healthy friendships. If you feel like one of your relationships is becoming detrimental to you—mentally, academically, or physically—don't be afraid to cut ties with that person. High school will be some of the most stress-inducing years of your life as you juggle a new, more burdensome set of responsibilities, but they should also be some of the most gratifying ones. Surround yourself with incredible friends who support you and, most importantly, remind you to enjoy these next four years."

(Candace Okumko, a senior at Oakland Mills High School, source link: https://superintendent.hcpss.org/2015/04/a -seniors-advice-to-incoming-freshmen/)

THRIVING FRESHMAN TIP #29

Go Out Of Your Way To Just Be Friendly!

Even if you're shy, when you enter classrooms full of
strangers, make it a habit to say "Hi!" to the person in the
desk beside you. Ask the student who sits in front of you
how he or she is doing. Then, put out your hand (or if
you're really shy, just put on a big smile) and introduce
yourself. Repeat the same process the next day and the
next, and soon you'll have some new friends. You'll begin
to feel like you really belong in that environment.

JOSHUA'S NOTES

I am generally a pretty shy person. I like to
think that I am super friendly but I don't often
initiate the conversations with people I meet.
However, I know intellectually that the kids
sitting next to me in class are just like me.
Most are nice kids, but they may struggle with

some level of shyness or insecurities. Typically, a gesture of friendship will always be welcome by kids with authentic personalities. Sure, there will be snobs but most people will respond to a friendly hello in a positive and polite manner.

Everybody loves a snack. So if you really want to make a new friend simply take out some candy for yourself and make sure the wrapper is a little loud. Trust me, everyone sitting around you will instantly whip their heads around into your direction. First, they want to see what you're eating and then, if it's good, they are hoping you offer them some of it. Whoever you share it with is going to instantly change their attitude about you. It's a great way to meet new people and I used it often during my freshman year.

Here is another tip but is much harder for shy people. Great friendships often begin with a compliment. So find something nice or flattering to say to new people you meet. The more people you know in your classes, the more comfortable and confident you will feel.

The research says it's that feeling of connectedness—or lack of it—that most often affects attendance rates. When you feel you're a part of something (like a class), you'll really want to be there. And, if you remember back a few pages, attendance rate can have a huge impact on not just a successful freshman year but ultimately a successful high school experience.

Want to know how important having good friends in high school can be? According to research done at the University of Virginia, your close friendships in high school more closely relate to the outcome of your high school years than does social acceptance (people.virginia.edu.)

In other words, having a good, supportive group of friends in high school will mean more to you and your future than whether you have the social acceptance of the whole school. So, it's to your benefit to have as large a group of positive, supportive people around you as possible but the quality of your friends trumps the quantity.

"I know this sounds strange, but as a kid, I was really shy. Painfully shy. The turning point was freshman year when I was the biggest geek alive. No one, I mean no one, even talked to me."- Jim Carrey

THRIVING FRESHMAN TIP #30

Hang With Kids Who Share Your Values and Vision For Their Future!

Every single graduating senior will tell you the same thing. Please, for the sake of your future success, take this one piece of advice and surround yourself with students who want to do well in school. Find friends who want to go to four-year colleges. They will motivate and inspire you, and you will do the same for them.

High school students, you will find, are quickly thrown into categories by your friends and frankly, by every other kid. While the whole world is trying to avoid stereotypes, the high school experience is largely characterized by the "types" of kids or the "groups of kids" that hang out together.

The important thing for you to think about is whether or not the people you spend the majority of your time associating with share a similar high school vision as you. Do they want to get good grades like you? Do they want to be involved in school activities like you? Do they want to go to college?

If you are like us, we really don't care much about the labels and we don't really care if we are labeled. What we mostly concern ourselves with is the character of the people we hang out with every day.

As you make these new friends please try to not to be something you are not. If you are a computer geek and you want to make friends with a football jock then do it as a computer geek. Supporting and lasting friendships begin with authenticity. If that girl thinks your interest in photography is lame then find a new friend. Don't drop the club because of her negative opinion.

> "Be who you are and say what you feel because those who mind don't matter and those who matter don't mind." –Dr. Suess

Even if you are super shy and the idea of saying hello to someone is just terrifying...don't worry. There is another sure fire way of making tons of friends without any effort at all.

THRIVING FRESHMAN TIP #31

Get Involved!

We have spent quite a bit of time sharing with you the importance of getting good grades, but grades are only part of the equation. It is critically important that you present yourself as a well-balanced and well-rounded student. You need to demonstrate some level of passion for other interests other than just the academics. Your participation in extracurricular activities is a great first step to showing that capability, but it brings the added benefit of you making a ton of new friends.

High schools are meccas for extracurricular activity. You know, sports...music...clubs? Your school probably has a multitude of these programs and most are free or come with a very small membership fee. Find the ones you find the most interesting, the ones that fit your talents. Soon you will find yourself in a room with like-minded people.

There is something that happens to people who are involved in clubs. They just come together. They build a loyalty to each other as they pursue similar ambitions or go through new experiences together. So if you want to make more friends without even thinking about it then get involved and watch your popularity soar.

Section

03

The Thriving Freshman
(Accelerating The Learning Curve)

Chapter 8

Thriving Is A Choice!

Now that you understand the importance of your freshman year in high school, you may feel a little—or very—stressed about this next step in your journey to being an adult. It's natural to feel some apprehension about any new endeavor, but once you are prepared for what lies ahead there should be no reason for feeling undue stress. Here are some tips and ideas on how to be that thriving freshman. Most of this information should resonate with you. You should be thinking, "Yes, I need to do that or act like that or think like that." However, for some of you this may be new information. We said it before, everyone is pretty much the same. We found literally hundreds of quotes from famous people who said they all experienced a great deal of anxiety and awkwardness their freshman year.

We think this comes from having very little information to help manage expectations. It's kind of like looking through a microscope for the first time. You know there are going to be some weird images that you have never seen before, but that knowledge does not prepare you for the amazing site of seeing microscopic creatures swimming around. It's like looking at a whole new world. Well, that is what high school is like. So we want to give you some additional information about what you can expect and what you can do to thrive in this new "high school" world. These tips will transform your freshman year if you have the discipline to follow the advice.

THRIVING FRESHMAN TIP #32

Start Thinking About Colleges This Year! Seriously, Don't Wait!

One thing you may want to research during this time is the particular requirements for each of the colleges you want to attend. Pick at least five colleges you think might be a good fit for you. You'll want to know more than just their grade requirements. Find out about the cost of tuition for each, and, if you are planning on living on campus, add the cost of room and board.

We know college may seem like a long way off. It really isn't it. Students are making their commitments earlier and earlier. You need to be on top of this game. Even if you don't know exactly where you want to go or what you want to study you can still start developing your college momentum today. Start by just looking around at nearby colleges. Do a little investigating. Arming yourself with some basic information like admission requirements will really help you stay focused on your high school goals.

It is critical that you understand that just getting into college is getting harder and harder. According to a recent article in *US News*, "There are more students considering college than in the past. And that means more people to compete with and more students to choose from." (Web. 30 July 2015.)

There are more students competing for spots in college now, so you'll be just one of thousands. Some of the top colleges receive *tens* of thousands of applications each year. AND they are accepting a smaller percentage of those applicants! You are not just competing with other high school students. Because the job market has been so terrible for the past 10 years, many working adults are going back to college to get retrained or learn new skills. That means more competition.

Harvard announced it had accepted just 5.9 percent (2,023 of 34,295) of the students applying for the class of 2018 (UChicago Consortium on Chicago School Research), and many other colleges admit 10% or less of their applicants (UChicago Consortium on Chicago School Research.) Even with colleges accepting fewer applicants, the number of people actually enrolling in college has increased at least 25% in the last three decades.

So, start your freshman year with a firm understanding you are not the only freshman looking toward college as a destination. Beginning with your first step into your first high school classroom, you'll need to stay focused. If your goal is to apply and be accepted at the college of your choice, you'll need to be sure you're taking the right steps.

We try to make life decisions by asking ourselves what good can come out of this decision or what bad can come out of this decision. If your life goals change and you ultimately decide you don't want to go to college you will not have hurt yourself in any way by getting good grades.

We can't leave a discussion of calculating college without also talking about college tuition. The price of college is soaring.

But, did you know the price of college is, in a large part, dependent on geography?

The lowest increase in tuition from the years 2008/9—2013/13 was in Missouri, where a 5% increase meant tuition cost $417 more, and during the same time period the highest was in Arizona, with an increase of 70% or $4,135 more. And although Georgia saw only a 65% increase, its tuition average of $7,823 was still above the national, which was $8,893 ("Tuition and Fees by Sector and State over Time".) And that's just for tuition!

According to the College Board website, you can add an average of $8,893 for room and board to the cost of tuition. And those textbooks you haven't worried too much about until now? What will buying a textbook mean once you're in college? Who knows? The Government Accountability Office notes from the years 2002—2012, there was an 82% increase in the cost of textbooks ("What the GAO Found").

Our advice is to investigate your local colleges and determine their costs and admission standards. You will almost immediately realize that college is cray expensive and it is not getting cheaper anytime soon. But don't get discouraged. Roughly two-thirds of full-time college students rely on some form of financial aid to help cover the cost of college. But we don't want you thinking about how you are going to pay for college right now. It is more important today that you focus all of your attention on making sure you have the grades and resume to get into college. We provide lots of strategies for affording college later in this book and in much greater detail in the other books in this series (i.e. Good Sophomore To Thriving Sophomore, Good Junior To Thriving Junior and Good Senior To Thriving Senior).

Get your grades as high as you can today because we are going to show you how to rely on those good grades for helping to cover the cost of college. Grants and scholarships are widely available and can really help make sure you can not only pay for college, but they can help make sure you don't graduate with tons of student loans.

And how do you qualify for grants and scholarships? One word: grades. So take some time before the first day of your freshman year to think about your future, particularly the next four years. Look at the requirements for the colleges that interest you, and then look at the courses you are scheduled to take your first year of high school.

Focus first on your core courses (English, math, science, and social studies). Are they at a level leading to the courses the colleges you're interested in attending say you need to have before you graduate? If not, you need to make some changes now. Most schools require parent involvement before making schedule changes and we know not all parents are..uh…completely involved.

That is okay, remember this is your life and so it is your responsibility to make sure you are doing things correctly. If you need to, schedule a meeting with your high school counselor to make sure you are tilting the table in your favor. They will be very helpful when they know you care about your future.

THRIVING FRESHMAN TIP #33

Take At Least One SAT or ACT Prep Class!

We already went over how important these tests are to your ultimate acceptance into that dream college. You need to perform well on these tests. Some high schools offer specific courses designed to prepare you for the various standardized tests. If yours does, we highly recommend that you try to fit it into your course schedule prior to taking the tests. If it doesn't, be sure to make the most of your core classes (English, math, social studies, and science.) You may also want to take one of the preparation classes offered by a for-profit franchise. Although most standardized tests allow for retesting, you don't want to retake the test too many times, especially if the scores are not improving. if you take the SAT 2-4 times and demonstrate a general improvement from test to test it will most often be seen as a positive by admission officers.

CHADNEY'S NOTES

I took the PSAT and scored terribly. I then took the SAT and scored a little better. My parents enrolled me in a standardized test course and my next SAT went up about 150 points. However, this was not good enough. So we hired a very expensive private tutor and the results were incredible. My final SAT score was 580 points higher than my first test. However, you need to understand, I studied my tail off. I knew I had to crack a very high bar to get into the Air Force Academy and I worked hard to get there. I think my parents spent about $3,000 or more in outside tutoring.

And while we're discussing the types of things colleges might require on their applications for submission, most colleges require some form of essay. Because you will be practicing essays all the time and as a THRIVING FRESHMAN you will be writing as if it were going to a college admission officer, you will be well prepared to do well on this part of the SAT. However, if you feel like your writing skills are below average you will want to get some tutoring. Our advice is to get that help by the end of your sophomore year. In Good Sophomore To Thriving Sophomore, we'll give you some incredible tips on how to write a killer essay that will stand out from the crowd of applicants.

THRIVING FRESHMAN TIP #34

Demonstrate Leadership Wherever You Can!

What if there's a club or activity you would like, but your school doesn't offer it? Ask how you can go about having one started. Usually, there will be an activities coordinator on your campus. If not, talk to your counselor.

Starting a new club demonstrates original thinking and it will have a meaningful impact on your college application. It demonstrates you have initiative. If you can get a lot of people involved in your new club you demonstrate a new level of achievement. If you can get other nearby schools to open similar clubs and conduct joint meetings, you have demonstrated an ability to achieve results, manage resources, and build consensus. This is a powerful story that can really distinguish your high school experience.

Having an extracurricular activity that really holds your interest is important for a number of reasons. First, it gives you a home, a place to belong, a community where you are with those who share your interests. Students who connect with this sense of community are less likely to drop out and more likely to do well in their classes.

Extracurricular activities also show college admission departments your interests. Being involved in more than just the academic side of high school shows you can manage your time. Colleges want students who contribute to a diverse student body experience. When you can demonstrate more dimensions than just great grades, you stand out. We had a friend who got into Harvard with a GPA that was less than a 4.0. However, he had lived two years in

Russia, spoke three languages, and ran a fitness blog with more than 12,000 subscribers.

The fact of the matter is getting good grades simply isn't enough. Everyone gets "good" grades. You have got to be proactive at developing the "whole person" aspect. You may have a solid 4.0 GPA, which is impressive on any standards, but it is not guaranteed that you will get into your "dream school." What happens when a college admissions counselor sees two transcripts with exactly the same classes and exactly the same grades? The answer is obvious; they will look for something to separate the two candidates. So do something! But more importantly do something you love! Do not just study. Separate yourself from the crowd. Whether that be writing a book, creating an app, playing for a team, starting a club, playing an instrument, getting a job; you have got do something more than just getting good grades.

To prove my point let's look at what I did with my high school career. Now, it is no secret

120

my grades were sub-par freshman and sophomore year. At that point in my life, it looked like I would have to go to a Junior College before getting into a four-year school...but that was not the case.

I decided to be proactive about developing the "whole person". So, from the summer of my sophomore year to the end of my senior year, I committed myself to achieving results that would separate my college application from students competing for the relatively small number of spots available.

I guarantee you there were smarter kids who applied to the same schools as me yet I received the acceptance letters. By the way, I applied to five universities and was accepted by all of them. Me, the student who blew it the first two years. Take my advice, grades don't tell enough of a story anymore to the admissions officers who are making the decisions.

Yes, grades are extremely important; however, don't just rely on grades to get you into college because they will not. Develop yourself so that when you have an interview with your college counselor they are just amazed at everything you have done and cannot help but send you the letter of acceptance.

Let's face it. Juggling various out-of-class obligations in addition to doing well with a full course load is a testament to the time management of any high school student which is why it will set you apart from others with GPAs similar to yours. So, if it can give you an advantage over others who don't participate in extracurricular activities, why not participate in doing something you enjoy.

THRIVING FRESHMAN TIP #35

Get Involved In Your Community!

Think about it: extracurricular doesn't mean it has to be school sponsored. You can also volunteer in the community. If you have a fondness for animals, you could volunteer at an animal shelter or work for a veterinarian. Is gardening your thing? Check with your local garden club to see if they have on-going projects needing your help. Whatever your interest, there is sure to be a place where your help is needed. An added benefit is you will be able to have some "me" time away from the books, and who doesn't want to be with others who share the same interests? It's a win-win situation.

You'll be able to participate in activities you enjoy while at the same time accumulating tangible evidence that you have one quality colleges covet more than high GPAs—commitment. They want to know you are able to follow through on commitments, stay the course, and stay in it for the long haul—all those old clichés showing you have what it takes to stay in college until you earn their degree. What they don't want is another drop-out statistic and showing you can stay involved, even when it's difficult, proves you have what it takes. Who knew doing something you really like could have such an impact on your future?

One last note on extracurricular involvement; colleges have become very aware of students who try to puff up their college applications months before they are due. Many students start clubs, join groups or go on mission trips right before they start applying to college. It totally transparent and at the end of the day the benefits really don't pay off. Colleges want students who demonstrate a consistency in their involvement. They genuinely want to know where your passion lies.

So our advice is the same as it is with your academics…start strong. Start that club this year. Start that foundation this year. Start that student charity this year…your freshman year. Stay with it all four years and beyond. Don't just do it because you think it will give you a one-time benefit because it probably won't. We found a bunch of information about how this kind of behavior is actually detrimental to the college acceptance process. One counselor even described it a kind of deceptive tactic.

There are literally hundreds of accomplishments you can achieve outside of school that would blow away college admission officers. If you just focus on achieving one significant thing each year you will have four meaningful things to talk about on your college application.

THRIVING FRESHMAN TIP #36

Achieve Something Significant Every Summer!

Don't waste summer. Your single best opportunities to improve our competitive admission qualifications will occur when school is out of session. We set achievement goals every summer. We always tried to align our goals with our future interests and the admission demands of our dream colleges.

I think I set the bar pretty high when I decided to pursue the military academies. When I read the admission brochures it looked like you had to be a dot-com genius, entrepreneur, leader, etc. to get into these schools. I wasn't. I knew I would need to demonstrate and stretch my comfort and capabilities in a compelling way for me to distinguish myself.

I began working to earn enough money to get intense athletic training in an effort to improve my soccer skills. I took the initiative to start a summer soccer camp for kids transitioning from AYSO to club soccer. I started writing and took classes at the nearby junior college. I took up photography and spear fishing and I started a small mobile application development company. All of these activities were things I wanted to do and because of that the achievement goals not overly challenging to accomplish. The fact is I enhanced my high school resume in a pretty powerful way doing things that I really loved to do.

My summers were awesome and educational and the summer activities I pursued allowed me to distinguish myself. If I know anything I know that it was not just my

GPA that got me into the U.S. Air Force Academy. It was my ability to activate resources and achieve something independent of my high school activities.

So take advantage of your summer. Play your video games at night but spend your days working towards goals that are of interest to you. Here are a few ideas:

- *Offer To Do A Free Internship At A Local Company Or Organization*
- *Take Extra Coursework At A Community College*
- *Train To Run A Marathon*
- *Take Up A Musical Instrument*
- *Volunteer At A Hospital Or Senior Center*
- *Start A Band Or Manage A Band*
- *Build An Mobile Application*
- *Start A Blog*
- *Make A Series Of Instructional Youtube Videos*
- *Start An Online Affiliate Business*
- *Write A Business Plan For Any Idea*
- *Write And Ebook*
- *Start A Foundation*
- *Get A Job*

"When planning your summer, it is important to think about what YOU want to do and accomplish this summer – not what you think might impress others. When you invest time in things you love, your engagement with the activity will be real and genuine. So relax... think about your summer "bucket list" and make time for learning, fun, family, friends, goofing off / sleeping in (within reason), personal engagement and making an impact."

(Lisa Micele, director of college counseling at the University of Illinois Laboratory High School in Urbana, Illinois, source link: *http://hereandnow.wbur.org/2015/06/17/summer -advice-for-teens*)

You are probably thinking to yourself that all of these ideas sound pretty cool, but you have no idea how to do any of them. That is the kind of thinking that will hold you back. Start by just Googling anyone of these topics. With just a little bit of effort, you will quickly find that you can easily do any one of these or a hundred others. The famous Chinese philosopher and poet Lao Tzu said "The journey of a thousand miles begins with the first step". So take that first step and just get started.

THRIVING FRESHMAN TIP #37

If You Fall Behind Get Help Immediately!

Don't think that you have some special ability to play catch up or that you will magically outperform on the next test even though the last three resulted in poor grades. The definition of insanity is doing the same thing over and over and expecting different results. If you put in time studying for a test and then performed poorly, the chances are you are going get the same result next time.

One of the biggest mistakes students make is getting a test back and then after learning which questions they answered incorrectly, they walk away with the false sense that they will not make that mistake again. Wrong! Nothing has changed. All that happened is that someone told you the correct answer. You did not develop a new strategy or method of studying that would prevent you from making the same mistake again.

All things being equal, however, you perform on your first tests and homework assignments will probably be your pattern the rest of the semester. The only way to improve is to change the way you study.

Our advice to you is to get help as early as possible. Every high school counselor and educator are trained for this challenge. In fact, it is one of their core employment functions. They have experience, ideas, and resources. Meet with them regularly and share with them you goals and struggles. Aside from your parents, your counselor is your biggest fan. Your success is their job fulfillment.

> "To put teens on a trajectory for success, college prep needs to start early......"
>
> (Ruth Lohmeyer, counselor at Lincoln Northeast High School in Nebraska, source link: http://www.usnews.com/education/blogs/high-school-notes/2013/09/09/use-all-4-years-of-high-school-to-prep-for-college   )

THRIVING FRESHMAN TIP #38

Know That We Are Rooting For You! Know That Your Parents Believe In You! Know That Every Teacher and Administrator Wants The Best For You!

We want you to be successful and we know you can. If this book has had one recurring piece of advice it is that you really need to do everything you can to start strong.

Playing catch-up is a recipe for serious problems. On the other hand, when you pull a high grade right out of the gate you build confidence and dramatically reduce your level of stress.

If you do find yourself falling behind get help quickly. We all have a tendency to "think" we know what to do and how to study to ensure we get the grades. It is time for you to be honest. Facts don't lie. If you are getting "C's" or worse on your tests and homework assignments then you do not know what to do or how to study. At least you haven't figured out the class that gave you the "C". You need to change something and you need to do it now and in dramatic fashion. You also need to realize that nobody is going to do it for you. This is on you and no one else. This is not a case where your teacher hates you (unless you gave them a reason to hate you.)

Take responsibility and take action. Get help. Change you study habits. Find more time each day to study. Join or start a study club. Act now because this quarter or semester is going to fly by and before you know it you are out of time.

The only way you can fix bad grades is to retake the class in the summer and there goes your summer.

Finally, understand that there is a college for every student and you will get into college. We want you to get into your dream college and if you follow our advice you will absolutely make that happen.

Welcome to the greatest time of your life. We are rooting for you.

Chad and Josh Hill

CITATIONS

"5 Innovative and Off Beat Ways to Pay for College." *The Fiscal Times.* Web. 4 Aug. 2015.

"7 Smart Ways to Pay for College." *Www.kiplinger.com.* Web. 4 Aug. 2015.

"7 Tips to Help Teens Successfully Transition to High School | Fox News." *Fox News.* FOX News Network, 29 July 2012. Web. 30 July 2015.

"10 Habits of Highly Effective Students." *Study Habits of Highly Effective Students.* Web. 3 Aug. 2015.

"20.pdf." *Scribd.* Web. 3 Aug. 2015. <https://www.scribd.com/doc/271371065/20-pdf>.

"Be Your Own Best Advocate." *Pacer Center Action Information Sheet.* Pacer Center, 2012. Web. 3 Aug. 2015.

"BullyPolice.org." *BullyPolice.org.* Web. 3 Aug. 2015.

"The Many Benefits of Breakfast." *WebMD.* WebMD. Web. 2 Aug. 2015.

"Preparing to Study: A Good Study Place." *Preparing to Study: A Good Study Place*. 2015. Web. 3 Aug. 2015.

"Qualities of a Successful College Student." *Qualities of a Successful Student*. Web. 3 Aug. 2015.

Song, Isabel. "How to Survive High School." *The Huffington Post*. TheHuffingtonPost.com. Web. 3 Aug. 2015.

"Ten Ways to Pay for College Now." *Forbes*. Forbes Magazine, 2015. Web. 4 Aug. 2015.

"The First Year of High School: A Quick Stats Fact Sheet." *National High School Center*. Betterhighschools.org, 1 Mar. 2007. Web. 30 July 2015.

"The Many Benefits of Breakfast." *WebMD*. WebMD. Web. 2 Aug. 2015.

"Tuition and Fees by Sector and State over Time." *Trends in Higher Education*. The College Board, 2015. Web. 30 July 2015.

"UChicago Consortium on Chicago School Research." *CCSR Publications*. Web. 3 Aug. 2015. <http://ccsr.uchicago.edu/publications/p78.pd>.

"U.S. ACT Exam Score Average Slips, but More Students College-ready, Report Says." *Best of Cleveland.com*. Associated Press. Web. 31 July 2015.)

Web. 3 Aug. 2015. <http://eric.ed.gov/?q=importance of 9th grade
year&ft=on&id=ED541362>.

Web. 3 Aug. 2015. <http://files.eric.ed.gov/fulltext/ED541362.pdf>.

Web. 3 Aug. 2015
<http://people.virginia.edu/~psykliff/pubs/publications/jill
_carlivati.doc>.

"What the GAO Found." *Higher Education: State Funding Trends of
Affordability*. US Government Accountability Office, 16 Dec. 2014. Web.
30 July 2015.

Willens, Michele. "Ninth Grade: The Most Important Year in High
School." *The Atlantic*. Atlantic Media Company, 1 Nov. 2013. Web. 3 Aug.
2015.

22782832R00075

Made in the USA
Columbia, SC
31 July 2018